The In-Between

The In-Between

A Play

Marcus Youssef

with a foreword by Carmen Aguirre

Study Guide included

Talonbooks

Talonbooks
9259 Shaughnessy Street, Vancouver, British Columbia, Canada v6p 6r4
talonbooks.com

Talonbooks is located on xʷməθkʷəy̓əm, Sḵwx̱wú7mesh, and səlilwətaʔɬ Lands.

First printing: 2022
Typeset in Minion
Printed and bound in Canada on 100% post-consumer recycled paper

Interior design by Typesmith
Cover illustration and design by andrea bennett

Talonbooks acknowledges the financial support of the Canada Council for the Arts, the Government of Canada through the Canada Book Fund, and the Province of British Columbia through the British Columbia Arts Council and the Book Publishing Tax Credit.

Rights to produce *The In-Between*, in whole or in part, in any medium by any group, amateur or professional, are retained by the author. Interested persons are requested to contact the author's agent: Colin Rivers, Marquis Entertainment, P.O. Box 47026, Eaton Centre, Toronto, on m5b 2p9; telephone: 416-960-9123, ext. 226; email: colin@mqent.ca.

Library and Archives Canada Cataloguing in Publication

Title: The in-between : a play / Marcus Youssef ; with a foreword by Carmen Aguirre.
Names: Youssef, Marcus, author. | Aguirre, Carmen, 1967- writer of foreword.
Identifiers: Canadiana 20210366753 | isbn 9781772012408 (softcover)
Subjects: lcgft: Drama.
Classification: lcc ps8597.o89 i5 2022 | ddc c812/.54—dc23

For my sister, Patricia, who found us

And Emma Tibaldo, who
contributes so much to this work

Foreword

In *The In-Between*, protagonist Lily, a North American high-school student, her crush Karim, and her best friend Brit contend with themes of xenophobia, racism, white supremacy, classism, poverty, and adult mental illness. All while navigating the destructive power of social media and their own quests for identity and belonging.

The tensions between class and race – Lily, Karim, and Brit are of different races and social classes – hang in the air throughout the play. Without being heavy-handed, it is in fact the backdrop for all the action. *The In-Between* takes us into the lives of these vastly different characters, who are all wrestling with the overarching teenage questions of *Where do I fit in? How do I fit in? Why am I in the world? How am I in the world?* And, most importantly, *How do I want to be in the world?*

Marcus Youssef has written multifaceted, current characters and immersed them in a rapidly changing world that they are struggling to keep up with. As they grapple with adult-sized ethical questions and choices – not to mention not knowing where your next meal is coming from or whether a white-supremacist gang is going to beat you up – they also contend with the universal teenage trials of bullying, loneliness, friendship, and first love. Seamlessly recreating the messiness of the real world, Marcus has put Lily and her friends inside it and forced them to deal with it in each of their flawed, human ways. These characters learn about conflict and how to resolve it, about loyalty, and about standing up for what you believe in. We watch them acquire coping skills, face moral dilemmas; we witness them start to find themselves and their own truths. They each begin to develop their belief system and how to articulate it, how to confront each other – and themselves – with care and respect.

Marcus does not shy away from tackling the minefields of racism and classism, bringing nuance and clarity to these interlocking systems through the lives of our teenage protagonists. In the end, *The In-Between* is a call for unity in the face of seemingly irreparable division. The play takes us into the depths of what looks like insurmountable conflict and offers us hope in its final moment. As a poor, brown, refugee kid myself, who confronted racism and classism while growing up in Vancouver in the 1970s, I applaud this brilliant, moving, funny, complicated story by my friend Marcus Youssef.

—CARMEN AGUIRRE

Playwright's Note

I began writing *The In-Between* in 2015 after becoming obsessed with the story of Ahmed Mohamed, a grade-nine student in Texas whose clock-making science project was mistaken for a bomb. A gawky fourteen-year-old science nerd inspires this reaction because of the associations the dominant culture makes based on the sound of his name, the colour of his skin, and his presumed religion. None of this is surprising, of course. But it was also flabbergasting. I then began to think about how different but equally ridiculous presumptions are projected onto low-income folks, based in this case on class. And then I hit on the central idea of the play itself, which really comes from a version of my own experience. It is the experience of a person who, for whatever reason, identifies with both sides of assumed binaries and so feels like they don't know which side they're supposed to be on. This for me is what makes *The In-Between* both a natural companion piece to my earlier play, *Jabber*, and an entirely different kind of exploration of difference and belonging and how those key paradigms play out in young people's lives.

—MARCUS YOUSSEF

The In-Between

Production History

The In-Between was commissioned and first produced from September 2018 to April 2019 by Geordie Theatre in Montréal, Québec, with the following cast and crew:

LILY	Qianna MacGilchrist
BRIT	Skyler Clark
KARIM	Sepehr Reybod

Director	Mike Payette
Dramaturge	Emma Tibaldo
Set and Costume Designer	Diana Uribe
Lighting Designer	Tim Rodrigues
Sound Designer	Rob Denton
Video Designer	Amelia Scott
Choreographer	Holly Greco
Props Master	Mathieu Cardin

The play was subsequently produced and toured both live and online to Young People's Theatre, Toronto, Ontario; Persephone Theatre, Saskatoon, Saskatchewan; and across the United States in 2021 and 2022.

The In-Between was developed in partnership with Playwrights' Workshop Montréal, with the support of the Cole Foundation.

Characters

LILY, Vietnamese Canadian, adopted as a baby and raised by a white Canadian family
BRIT, white, lives with her low-income single mom
KARIM, Lebanese emigrant whose parents work in tech
(All are fifteen- to sixteen-ish)

MS. CHAN, a teacher, and PRINCIPAL TENDERS appear only in voice-over on the PA. Their lines can be recorded by any two of the three actors in the production.

BENNIE participates in text messages but does not appear onstage.

Settings

St. Mary's Secondary School, where an increasingly large group of Middle Eastern refugees has arrived over the last few years

The Hill, a spot overlooking the school where kids hang out

Brit's apartment

Production Design

In the original productions, projections were used for nearly all of the dialogue that is communicated via text and social media. This worked well and was my original intention. It is also possible to consider other ways of enacting these. The stage directions reflect the first production's approach.

Note on Overlapping Dialogue: A double slash, //, is used in this text to indicate a point where one character's dialogue overlaps another's.

Top: Qianna MacGilchrist and Skyler Clark in *The In-Between*, by Marcus Youssef, Geordie Theatre, October 2021. Photo by Andrée Lanthier.

Bottom: Sepehr Reybod, Qianna MacGilchrist, and Skyler Clark in *The In-Between*, by Marcus Youssef, Geordie Theatre, October 2021. Photo by Andrée Lanthier.

Scene One

*Maybe: audio or documentary footage of kids in a
school. The following is punctuated by a smartphone's
camera clicks and/or Snapchat sounds.*

LILY talks to the audience.

LILY

When I was a kid, like, in grade eight, this whole thing happened
on social media. Between these two girls. They were both my
friends, kind of. It was just stupid at first, but then got intense.

We had this English teacher who always acted like she was
everybody's friend. Which she kind of was, but anyway. We were
all in her class and out of nowhere she stopped talking about *To
Kill a Mockingbird* or whatever and was like, "I know I'm old, but
how about this? When people are sharing stuff online and you
want to respond, what if you write out whatever you want to say or
do, but then don't post it? What if you wait a day or two and then
decide if it's still something you want everybody to see?"

Everybody was like, uh, whatever. I thought it was kind of dumb.

Until the last little while. When this whole thing about racism
happened between my best friend and this guy I like and other
kids too. Refugee kids. From, you know, Syria and stuff. There's a
bunch of them in our school now.

I wrote what I wanted to say down. I don't know if I should share
it or not. This isn't posting, I know, but...

It's what happened when I found myself where I feel like I always
am, stuck in the middle, in-between. Not sure what I think,
or whose side I'm on. Or even who I really am.

5

Scene Two

Projection: memes / texts / social media (Instagram, Snapchat) punctuated by audio and/or music. From the first production:

> *Instagram meme: image of Muslim kid made to look like a terrorist*
>
> *Video: news footage of the aftermath of the 2017 Québec City mosque shooting*
>
> *Video: other Islamophobic or Proud Boys or alt-right–related footage*
>
> *Instagram meme: insulting white "redneck" with the caption, "HELLO MY NAME IS BENNIE"*
>
> *Instagram meme: Afghanistan, very rural, poor, with the caption, "CANADA IN 2025. Too many immigrants!!!!!!"*
>
> *Image: poor whites looking "trashy"*
> *with Arabic text:* شوف! انا شفت صورة
> لبيني وعائلتو
> *then "Hahahahaha!"*

… and multiple other images.

A climax of sound and image. Music. Transition. Maybe it's dance. Maybe something else. Snapchat sounds? Maybe they continue as the PA begins.

Scene Three

School. Midday.

*LILY has a spare. BRIT and LILY are in the cafeteria
before lunch. LILY wears Star Wars goggles on her head.
She is working on something. BRIT is bored. There's
room for them to ad-lib or goof around a little during
the announcements.*

MS. CHAN (*voice-over on the PA*)
Mrs. Pattifong would like to say thank you to everyone who
entered the anti-bullying logo competition. Congratulations to
Letisha Winterson, who wins a Starbucks gift certificate. Her
design will also be featured on buses and subways across the city.

Sound of MS. CHAN moving away from the mic.

MS. CHAN (*voice-over on the PA*)
Do you want me to read this?

*Sounds of shuffling paper. Ms. Chan's voice comes back
fully on mic; she reads, but she clearly hasn't rehearsed.*

"In regards to the incidents that have taken place on social media,
we remind students that threats and intimidation are against
the school code of conduct. Those who break laws will face
the consequences, including comments made on the internet."
Is that okay?

More shuffling noise. The voice on the PA changes.

7

PRINCIPAL TENDERS (*voice-over on the PA*)
Yes. Thanks, Ms. Chan, great job as always. It's Principal Tenders
here, I just want to add that what you say matters, right? Even if
it's on a screen. This school has experienced a lot of changes in
the last few years. We've welcomed a lot of newcomers who have
come from a very difficult place. Let me be clear, all are welcome
at St. Mary's. Our diversity is our strength. Take care of each other,
okay? (*to Ms. Chan*) Do you want the mic back?

BRIT
Please just take them off.

LILY
Why?

BRIT
They're embarrassing.

LILY
Nobody even cares.

    BRIT grabs at the goggles, half playing.

LILY
Brit, don't!

    BRIT gives up.

BRIT
Oh my god, I'm so *bored.*

LILY
Do your science.

    BRIT groans.

8

LILY
Just do it.

BRIT
(*imitating*) "Just do it."

LILY
It's so easy.

BRIT
I have Ms. Derriere. I can't do homework for a teacher whose name means "butt."

LILY
You need it to graduate. You have to finish high school.

BRÍT
Why?

LILY
Because.

BRIT
Good answer. So convincing.

> *Beat.*

BRIT
You're coming over tonight, right?

LILY
I'm not sure.

BRIT
You have to. Okay?

LILY
Is something going on?

BRIT
No.

LILY
Really?

BRIT
(*imitating her, making fun of her concern*) "Really?"

LILY
Your mom's still working?

BRIT
Yes.

LILY
I have to finish my socials essay. It's due tomorrow.

BRIT
Do it now.

LILY
I am doing it!

BRIT
Liar.

BRIT grabs her paper.

BRIT
I knew it. Star-nerds fanfic. Oh my god. (*reading*) "The snow battered the two opponents as each struggled to gain mastery. Rey

had never touched a lightsabre in her life." Oooohh – touch my
lightsabre, Rey!

LILY
Shut up!

BRIT
You wrote it. (*reading*) "'I can show you the ways of the force!'
Kylo Ren declared, trying to tempt Rey as he pushed against her."

Ohh, push against me Kylo Ren, push against me!

LILY
That's not what it's about!

BRIT
(*reading*) As if. "Their locked blue-and-red sabres cast an eerie
glow around them. 'The Force,' Rey breathed. 'The Force.'"

LILY
I got thirty comments on the last chapter.

BRIT
For real?

LILY
Sixty-four new follows. One thousand three hundred views. Like,
ten from Mexico.

BRIT
They should see you in your little outfit. Joking. This is actually
really good.

LILY

I'm going to send it to this Star Wars fanfic contest. The winners get to go to Comic Con. In Los Angeles. They pay for your plane and everything.

BRIT

You gonna dress up?

LILY

At Comic Con, everybody does.

BRIT

As Padme?

LILY

Rey, not Padme. Rey is cool.

BRIT

Dude. Nothing about *Star Wars* is cool.

LILY

In one comment a guy said he thinks I'm good enough to write the actual movies.

BRIT

I bet he just wants in your pants –

LILY

Ewww!

BRIT

Your *Padme* pants.

BRIT playfully grabs LILY's goggles.

LILY
Shut up! Hey! What are you doing?

BRIT pulls out her phone and goes to take a selfie of them together. It's possible that we see it.

BRIT
Check it out.

BRIT has added filters to the selfie, giving them both classic Vietnamese farmer hats.

BRIT
Look.

At some point LILY gets the phone.

LILY
Very funny.

BRIT
You look like your ancestors. You shouldn't go to Comic Con as Rey. You should go as a Chinese rice farmer.

LILY
Vietnamese. Duh.

BRIT
That's what I meant. What do they call that hat thing anyway?

LILY
Who knows? Maybe "a hat."

BRIT
It actually makes you look pretty.

LILY

It actually makes me look like an idiot.

> *BRIT tries to grab the phone from LILY. They tussle, having fun. KARIM enters.*

BRIT

You have to give it to me. I'm using the Force.

> *BRIT stops because she sees KARIM.*

BRIT

Oh my god, it's that's refugee kid again. What's his name?

LILY

Karim.

BRIT

You hear what he said to Bennie?

LILY

No.

BRIT

It was so racist. He's staring at us.

LILY

He's not a refugee. He's lived here since grade two.

BRIT

How do you even know that?

LILY

He told me.

BRIT
He looks like a refugee.

LILY
Brit.

BRIT
What?

LILY
I told him I'd give him my chem homework. He missed class because he's got this, like, paid apprenticeship. With a real tech company. I think his parents work for Google.

KARIM comes up to them.

KARIM
Yo.

BRIT
(*imitating*) "Yo."

LILY gives her a sharp look.

BRIT
What? He's like, "Yo."

KARIM
So?

LILY
(*to KARIM, about class*) You didn't miss much.

KARIM
Did he give out worksheets?

LILY

I don't get how teachers think doing worksheets helps you learn anything.

KARIM

I know. I think they use them so they won't have to do any work. Which is pretty ironic, since it's called a *work*sheet.

BRIT

What are you even talking about?

LILY

Ionic bonds.

KARIM

I know. What are you doing for your physics project?

LILY

Oh, I don't know yet. What about you?

KARIM

I don't know either. But I need it to be really good. I told the CEO of the place I'm doing the apprenticeship, and she was like, "Impress us."

BRIT

This is the stupidest conversation I've ever heard.

KARIM

Brit, right?

BRIT

Yeah.

KARIM
What science are you in?

BRIT
Who cares?

KARIM
So, like, basic.

LILY
Basic is a lot more challenging than you think.

KARIM
Then why do they call it "basic"?

LILY hands KARIM the homework.

LILY
Here. Make a mistake or something. So she knows it's not mine.

KARIM
(*flirting*) I don't make mistakes.

LILY
That's not what I heard.

KARIM
Liar.

LILY
I never lie.

BRIT
(*to LILY*) Seriously?

KARIM
Do you want to go for lunch? Like, just you and me?

LILY glances at BRIT.

LILY
I can't. Sorry.

LILY holds up the Star Wars story.

LILY
Homework.

KARIM
Oh.

BRIT
She's lying. That's not homework. It's Star Wars fanfic.

KARIM
You're into Star Wars?

LILY
Sometimes. I do have a ton of homework. Maybe another time.

KARIM
Cool. See you in physics.

KARIM looks at them both and leaves.

Beat.

LILY
Oh my gosh, what was that?

BRIT
I know, right? What a simp.

LILY
No, why were you so rude?

BRIT
What are you talking about? He basically said I was stupid.

LILY
You started it. "Yo."

BRIT
He's a total dick. He called Bennie "white trash."

LILY
No he didn't.

BRIT
To his face.

LILY
How do you even know?

BRIT
Bennie told me.

LILY
As if.

BRIT
He did. Last night. We were chilling in the park.

LILY
You were hanging out with Bennie?

BRIT

I ran into him and his friends. He just started talking to me. Weird, huh?

Beat.

LILY

What about that T-shirt he wore? Remember? It literally said "White Power."

BRIT

Pride. It said "White Pride." There's a big difference. And he got suspended for that. Wearing a T-shirt! That's, like, censorship.

LILY

Bennie failed three grades. He's in grade eleven and he's, like, twenty years old.

BRIT

That's total BS. He failed one grade. And that wasn't his fault. He was messed up because of stuff that was going on his life. Like they were going to fail me, in grade five, remember? Until the teacher decided they didn't want to have to teach me again, so they just passed me anyway.

LILY

That's not what happened.

BRIT

Basically. Not everybody has two perfect parents who give them every little thing they want.

LILY hands BRIT an envelope.

BRIT

We're fine.

LILY

Take it. My mom and dad want you to. They care about you.

BRIT

I told you. My mom's working.

LILY

Just to help out.

BRIT takes the envelope.

BRIT

You are coming over tonight, right?

LILY

For sure.

BRIT

She always asks about you. Sometimes I think she wishes you were her kid, instead of me.

LILY

That's not true.

BRIT

I wish you were her kid, too. Joking. She just always cheers up a little, that's all. When you're around.

LILY

It's not starting again, is it?

BRIT
No.

LILY
I'll come by after dinner.

BRIT
Thanks. You do look pretty in that weird Chinese hat.

LILY
Vietnamese!

BRIT
(*joking, maybe an eye roll – it's a moment of connection*) Whatever.

    LILY leaves.

Scene Four

Later. LILY *texts and Snapchats with both* KARIM *and* BRIT. *These are projected.*

KARIM
hey

its karim

LILY to KARIM
"yo"

KARIM
haha how r u?

LILY to KARIM
good

KARIM
cool

BRIT
yo

LILY to KARIM
haha

BRIT SNAPCHAT
my mom's fat butt

KARIM
uh …

BRIT SNAPCHAT
im a cat

LILY to **KARIM**
sorry with some people

BRIT
hahahahaha

KARIM
who?

LILY to **KARIM**
just people

BRIT
where u?

LILY to **BRIT**
home

BRIT
doing HOMEWORK???

KARIM
mysterious …

LILY to **BRIT**
ya

LILY to **KARIM**
haha

LILY to BRIT
your mom home?

KARIM
np talk later?

LILY to KARIM
nows ok

LILY to BRIT
Is she?

KARIM
k

BRIT
who cares

LILY to KARIM
what r u doing?

KARIM
now?

LILY to KARIM
ya

KARIM
nothing

BRIT
what are u doing?

LILY to BRIT
i told you. homework

LILY to KARIM

i need my science back

KARIM

oh ok

LILY to KARIM

want to meet?

KARIM

ya!

LILY to KARIM

to get my science i mean

omg so awkward

BRIT sends a picture of herself being soooo bored.

KARIM

no

LILY to KARIM

no?

KARIM

yes i mn. lets meet

BRIT

how BORING U R!

BRIT

jkjkjkjk

LILY to KARIM

here?

LILY to BRIT

KARIM

the hill?

BRIT

when u coming?

LILY to BRIT

soon!

😊

LILY to KARIM

👍

Beat.

BRIT looks behind her.

BRIT

everything is so MESSED

BRIT deletes "MESSED."

LILY to KARIM

ok. after dinner

BRIT

she won't get out of bed

27

KARIM

BRIT deletes "she won't get out of bed." She types.

BRIT

crying nonstop

BRIT deletes "crying nonstop."

LILY to KARIM

BRIT

im scared

BRIT deletes "im scared."

BRIT

BRIT deletes all.

28

Scene Five

LILY and KARIM are at the edge of a park, not far from school.

KARIM
This is where I come when I skip.

LILY
You don't skip.

KARIM
I do. Sometimes.

LILY
Never chem.

KARIM
Maybe that's 'cause you're there.

LILY
Are you joking?

KARIM
I don't know. (*trying to be cool*) Am I? (*backtracking*) You know what, I'm not sure if I am or not.

LILY
I think you are.

KARIM shows LILY his phone.

KARIM

Check this out. My dad just bought it.

LILY

A Tesla?

KARIM

The SUV.

LILY

Woah.

KARIM

He'll never let me near it.

LILY

Are you, like, Syrian?

KARIM

No. Why?

LILY

Just wondering. Brit said you were.

KARIM

She's wrong. My family's from Beirut. It's a city in Lebanon. Which is next to Syria, but way different. It's pretty messed now, though. A while ago, there was this massive explosion in the harbour, it basically ruined everything.

LILY

It's weird how all those refugee kids arrived at the school all at once.

KARIM
Tell me about it.

LILY
You're different from them.

KARIM
What do you mean?

LILY
Just, like, they're really poor.

KARIM
They're not all poor.

LILY
They came with nothing.

KARIM
But the people who can get out of Syria and places like that are often, like, the doctors and lawyers, because they're the ones who can afford it and know people in Canada and stuff.

LILY
You're rich.

KARIM
Not rich.

LILY
A Tesla SUV costs, like, a hundred thousand dollars.

KARIM
It's a lease.

LILY
Did you call Bennie "white trash"?

KARIM
Have you seen the crap he posts?

LILY
Yeah.

KARIM
Somebody needs to shut him up. I'm sorry, but I'm sick of it.
Refugees aren't any different than anyone else.

LILY
They are a little different.

KARIM
How?

LILY
I just mean, like, literally. They don't speak English.

KARIM
Some of them do. A lot of them speak, like, five languages. Because
they've had to live in so many countries.

LILY
It's not an insult. They are really loud. Like, in the halls.

KARIM
Everybody's loud in the halls.

LILY
Honestly, they're louder.

KARIM
Okay, but that's just – that's because they're speaking Arabic, and you're not used to it. So you notice it more. And people from the Middle East, they talk a lot with their hands, all the time, like this: (*demonstrating with the phrases, gesticulating a lot*) "Hey, how's it going?" "Oh my god, you suck."

LILY
You have really nice hands.

KARIM
What?

LILY
Oh my gosh, I can't believe I just said that.

KARIM
So random. But whatever. You, uh, you have really nice hands, too.

LILY
Uh, thanks.

    Beat.

LILY
Awkward.

KARIM
So, like, what are you?

LILY
What do you mean?

KARIM
Are you, like, Chinese, or ...?

LILY

I'm Canadian.

KARIM

Yeah, but what else?

LILY

Nothing else.

KARIM

Yes, you are. I mean, like, your family.

LILY

My family is Canadian.

KARIM

You know what I mean.

LILY

No, they are. My parents are both white. I was adopted.

KARIM

Seriously?

LILY

From Vietnam. I lived in an orphanage there until I was six
months old. Then my parents went there from Canada and
adopted me.

KARIM

That's intense.

LILY

Not really. For me, it's normal.

KARIM
What about your Vietnamese family?

LILY
I don't have a Vietnamese family.

KARIM
You must have one.

LILY
Yeah – duh.

KARIM
Don't you want to know who they are?

LILY
I don't really care.

KARIM
For a long time, I didn't think it mattered where my family was from. But then I started to realize. It really matters. Because of morons like Bennie. It's all white supremacists see.

LILY
Cool.

KARIM
Did I say something wrong?

LILY
No.

KARIM
You sure?

LILY
(*lying*) Yes. Do you have my homework?

KARIM
Yeah.

KARIM hands it to LILY.

KARIM
I made a couple mistakes. On purpose.

LILY
Thanks.

LILY gets a text. She looks at it.

KARIM
Is homework really the reason you wanted to meet?

LILY looks at KARIM.
Beat.

LILY
Karim, I like you.

KARIM
I like you too. I have – for a long time.

LILY
But it's complicated.

KARIM
It doesn't have to be. Come on.

LILY
Where?

KARIM
Top of the Hill.

      LILY looks at her phone.

LILY
I told Brit I'd come over.

KARIM
Say you're busy.

LILY
It's not that simple.

KARIM
Why?

LILY
Her mom is... kind of messed up.

KARIM
How?

LILY
They're super broke.

KARIM
Doesn't she have a job?

LILY
For minimum wage.

KARIM

She should go back to school, so she can get a better one.

LILY

This is, like, kind of a secret but … Brit's mom has these episodes sometimes. It's like depression, I guess. Or something. She won't get out of bed and, like, cries. Like, a lot. It freaks Brit out.

KARIM

Then I guess you should go.

LILY

Brit says it helps. Her mom really likes me. 'Cause I'm so "good" or whatever. Then Brit disappears and I end up talking to her mom all night.

KARIM

That's weird.

LILY

I know. Honestly, I don't want to. It's just, like, so exhausting. I don't know how Brit can live with it. Don't tell anyone this, okay?

KARIM

I won't.

LILY

My parents give them money sometimes. Because her mom's always bailing on her jobs. You can't tell anyone I told you that.

KARIM

I promise. You can trust me.

LILY

I'm just, like, the kind of person, you know, who always feels like they have to take care of everybody else.

KARIM

Yeah. Sounds like maybe you are.

LILY takes KARIM's hand.

LILY

Let's go.

LILY leads the way out.

Scene Six

BRIT at home. She texts.

BRIT to LILY
> why u not answering?

BRIT waits. She looks behind her.

BRIT
(*to her mom, who is offstage*) I'll be there in a minute! If you're
hungry, there's baked beans on the counter!

BRIT texts.

BRIT to LILY
> its almost 8. where are u???????

BRIT gets up and walks to the door. She listens.

BRIT
(*to her mom*) No, I didn't steal it, Mom. It's fine. A kid owed me
money. They paid me back.

BRIT texts.

BRIT to LILY
> tx for the $$. bought food.

BRIT
(*to her mom*) I'll be down in a minute. I swear.

BRIT texts.

BRIT to **LILY**

> tonight i really need my best friend.

BRIT doesn't send it.

Scene Seven

LILY and KARIM are just reaching the top of the Hill.

LILY
I haven't been to the Hill in a long time. We used to come up here in grade eight. It was, like, this big deal.

KARIM
I remember.

LILY
You do?

KARIM
Like I said, I've liked you for a long time.

LILY
I love how it feels like we're in another world.

KARIM
(*pressing his fingers together, squinting through them*) School looks so little.

LILY
Like a toy or something. Kids in the field, they're like ants.

LILY
What are you doing?

KARIM
Crushing them all. I'm pretending it's Bennie and all his dumb-ass friends.

LILY gives him a look.

LILY
You shouldn't say stuff like that.

KARIM
Why not?

LILY
It freaks people out.

KARIM
What does?

LILY
Just, like, making threats.

KARIM
Because I'm Muslim?

LILY
I'm not saying it's right, but it does.

KARIM
I was joking.

LILY
I'm just saying.

LILY holds up her phone. We may see the image projected.

LILY
Did you snap this?

*It's a mean picture of "white trash" with the caption
"Hello my name is Bennie!"*

KARIM
So? It was after Bennie tagged my friend Tarek on this.

*A picture of war in Afghanistan with the caption
"CANADA IN 2025. Too many immigrants!!!!!"*

KARIM
V.P. called my parents. They totally freaked out. My dad was like,
why are you even involved in this? I was like, if I don't stand up
to them, nobody will. You know what's really ironic? My parents
don't like me hanging out with refugees. Because they're afraid
people will think we're like them. They've spent their whole lives
trying to prove to everybody that they're white.

LILY
Yeah.

KARIM
Right?

LILY
Say something in Arabian.

KARIM
Arabian? Oh my god. It's called "Arabic," not "Arabian."

LILY
Okay, fine, I'm sorry!

KARIM
I'm just bugging you. Why?

LILY
I just want to hear you speak it.

KARIM
You sure it's not going to scare you?

LILY
Shut up!

KARIM
(*in Lebanese Arabic*)

أنا فعلاً حبيت فيلم *The Last Gedi*.

ānā f'lā ḥbyt fylm *The Last Gedi*.*

What do you think it means?

LILY
How am I supposed to know? Something about *The Last Jedi*?

KARIM
"I really like the movie *The Last Jedi*."* I thought you'd like that.

> *KARIM pulls out his phone.*

(*reading*) "Rey's teeth grit together and she convulses, held in by her restraints."

---

* Update the movie title as necessary. Consult with the playwright if you want suggestions.

45

LILY

Oh my god, no, stop!

KARIM

I knew it was you. "The Force hold he has on her intensifies, scorching a path toward her distant, locked-away memories. No!"

LILY

I said stop!

KARIM

It's awesome. "Force power rushes back at him, blasting his mind. Then his own memories flash into existence; his loneliness and pain, his own remorse and guilt." Lilyfan003.

LILY

How'd you find it?

KARIM

It wasn't hard. Found some pictures, too.

LILY

Oh my god.

KARIM

No, it's awesome. I think cosplay is hot.

LILY

Shut up! It's not sexual.

KARIM

I still think it's hot.

LILY
If I win this contest, I might get to go to Comic Con. In Los
Angeles. It's so warm there you can swim in December.

KARIM
I bet you will win.

LILY
I don't know.

KARIM
I do.

    Beat.

KARIM
You should find your Vietnamese family.

LILY
Why?

KARIM
To learn about your culture.

LILY
If my parents are even alive, they probably don't speak English.

KARIM
They could be famous Vietnamese movie stars.

LILY
If they were movie stars, why would they give me up for adoption?

KARIM
Good point.

*LILY looks at her phone. We see that **BRIT** is texting,*
but not what she's writing.

KARIM
Brit?

*A text from **BENNIE** to **BRIT**, projected.*

BENNIE to BRIT
yo

LILY
Yeah.

BRIT to BENNIE
yo

KARIM
You're too good for her.

LILY
No, I'm not.

KARIM
Too nice. Too smart. Too cute.

BRIT erases her text.

KARIM
That's what I think.

*LILY puts away her phone and moves closer to **KARIM**.*

LILY
Ef it.

KARIM
Ef it?

We see BRIT's and BENNIE's texts.

BRIT to BENNIE
hey bennie

LILY
It's what I said. In case you hadn't noticed, I'm a total nerd.

KARIM
I noticed.

BENNIE to BRIT
chillin with lily?

LILY
This is for me.

LILY moves really close to KARIM.

BRIT
na. shes doin homework.

KARIM
For you?

LILY
Yeah.

BENNIE
she aint home

LILY kisses KARIM. Maybe she pulls out her goggles and puts them on him. Music. LILY kisses KARIM again.

BRIT
she isnt?

Sound of a photo being taken. Snap. BRIT erases "isnt."

BRIT
she aint?

BENNIE
saw em in the woods together

LILY and KARIM exit together.

BENNIE
lily karim

BRIT doesn't respond.

BENNIE
guess theyre going out

BRIT
wtf

BENNIE texts BRIT a picture of Lily and Karim making out.

BENNIE
its what they do

BENNIE
take away whats ours

Scene Eight

BRIT at home. She hears something and goes to her bedroom door.

BRIT
Mom.

Jesus, Mom. Stop crying. What is going on?

Lily's on her way. She said she's sorry she hasn't been by in a while and she wants to hang out with us.

Mom, stop crying. You're good.

Everything's going to be fine. Just stop.

Please. For once. God, why can't you just be okay?!

Scene Nine

LILY and BRIT are in the school hallway. The next day.

LILY

Hey, I've been looking for you.

BRIT

Oh yeah.

LILY

Is everything okay?

BRIT laughs.

LILY

I'm sorry I didn't make it over last night. I was just so busy. I lost track of the time.

BRIT

Did you get all your homework done?

LILY

Uh, yeah.

BRIT

I just want to be sure. That's why you "lost track of time," right? Because you were *home*. Doing *home*work. At *home*.

LILY

Uh, yeah.

BRIT
You know what's cool? How, like, "ho" and "home" are kind of, like, basically the same word.

LILY
What are you talking about?

> *BRIT shows LILY the picture of her and Karim kissing.*

LILY
Brit.

BRIT
Don't worry.

LILY
I'm really sorry I bailed on you. Okay?

BRIT
No, it's good. Now I know the truth.

LILY
What do you mean?

> *KARIM enters.*

BRIT
You care more about some Muzzie refugee than your best friend.

LILY
Don't call him that.

BRIT
(*imitating, mean*) "Don't call him that." (*to KARIM*) Watch your step.

KARIM
Excuse me?

BRIT
You heard me.

> *BRIT leaves, pushing past KARIM.*

KARIM
What's her problem?

LILY
She's pissed.

KARIM
Why?

LILY
(*irritated that he doesn't immediately know*) Last night.

KARIM
It's none of her business.

LILY
I know.

KARIM
I, uh, I got you something.

> *KARIM hands BRIT a Darth Vader stuffie. He leaves his backpack somewhat open. There's something else in it. A bit of it may be sticking out.*

LILY

Karim. That's so sweet. Oh my god, why is everything so effing messed up?

KARIM

If I'm honest? Because Brit is a racist.

LILY

Brit's not a racist. She's my oldest friend. She's just jealous.

KARIM

I know you guys go way back. But you have to stand up to hate. Believe me, I know. I've had to learn the hard way.

LILY

What do you mean?

KARIM

Bennie and them. All that white-power crap. If you don't push back, they just keep pushing you around.

LILY

His T-shirt said "White Pride."

KARIM

It's a dog whistle. Gaslighting. So it's the exact same thing. What do you think they say about you? Behind your back? You're not white, remember?

LILY

I know.

LILY gestures to KARIM's backpack.

LILY
What's that?

KARIM realizes it's open. He scrambles to close it.

KARIM
Nothing. It's for physics.

LILY
What is it?

KARIM
It doesn't matter. I'm going to grab some food. Do you want to come?

LILY
I'm not hungry.

KARIM
Come anyway. Come to the caf with me.

LILY
Not right now.

KARIM
Because of Brit?

LILY
You don't understand.

KARIM
No, I think maybe I do. But whatever. You should do what you want.

KARIM leaves.

Scene Ten

LILY talks to the audience, narrating the scene. At some point BRIT and KARIM enter. They're in the caf.

LILY
They both went to the caf. It's really small. They built it when the school was supposed to have three hundred kids. Now there's a thousand. Only about thirty are refugees, but... whatever.

I stood in the back out of sight. I just... watched.

Bennie was there with some grade elevens. It's always the same. Asian kids sit in the middle, First Nations kids at the far end, nerds on the floor in the back, and Bennie and his crew by the door.

But not this time.

This time, Brit goes up to Bennie and says something. And he laughs. Then they both get up and go over to where Karim and a bunch of the refugee kids are about to sit.

BRIT
This is our table.

KARIM
What are you talking about?

BRIT
It's our table. We were here first.

KARIM
No, you weren't.

BRIT

Yes, we were.

KARIM

I was literally here before you.

LILY

And then some girl says actually the First Nations were here first and then this First Nations girl Kim raises her fist and goes "It's true, *bitches* – we were!!" and a bunch of kids laugh.

BRIT

Whatever. We're here now.

KARIM

We always eat here. You've got your spot.

BRIT

Not today.

LILY

Everything got quiet. Some grade nines start pointing, whispering, "Look!"

BRIT

I said, "move." Muzzie.

LILY

Some other kids laughed. It's what Bennie and them call the refugee kids, because they're Muslim.

KARIM

What'd you call me?

BRIT
Muzzie.

KARIM
Oh okay, because I thought you said "nazi." Which would mean you're talking about yourself.

LILY
A few people laugh, because that doesn't really make sense. But then somebody – I don't know who – says, "Maybe they had the right idea, the nazis." I don't think it was Brit. I think it was Bennie. And somebody else laughs. And some other kids go, "Ooooohhhhh ... " And somebody else says, "Shut up." And some grade nines start chanting, "Nazi, nazi." Just because they're in grade nine.

BRIT shoves KARIM.

KARIM
Don't you dare touch me!

BRIT
Then make me stop!

KARIM
I don't hit girls.

BRIT
I bet you don't.

LILY
And then Brit moves close to Karim. Too close. They're all on their feet, in each other's faces. Shoulders back, chests sticking out, like chickens.

BRIT

Why don't you go back where you came from?!

KARIM

This *is* where I came from!

BRIT

No, it's not. You don't belong here, Muzzie.

> *LILY comes out of the shadows, joining the scene.*

LILY

Stop! Both of you, stop it!

> *Beat.*

LILY

(*talking to the audience*) And they both stop – and turn. Because the voice they hear, what they see ... is me.

Once, when I was a kid, my parents took me to this magic show. A magician put his assistant in a box with her head coming out one side and her legs sticking out the other. Then he pulled out this giant saw and cut the box in half. I know it's a dumb trick, but I remember thinking, how come she's smiling? Why doesn't somebody do something? Some guy in a purple suit is *sawing her in half.*

> *Loud, angry music. LILY turns and bolts. Maybe a video and/or audio like this one, abstracted, grainy: ABC News, "Students Taunt Minority Classmates: 'Build the Wall,'" YouTube, November 10, 2016, youtu .be/ewbpQEGwxQY. Maybe likes and smiles and angry faces, etc., floating through it, as per Instagram Live or Facebook Live.*

Texts, memes, and Snaps:

nicely dun brit!!!!!

Redneck meme

Gif: movie terrorist running in fear

Meme: woman in a burka: "Ridiculously Photogenic Muslim"

Ahmed the clock kid: and for my next class project

Etc.

Music. Transition. Maybe this continues as the PA begins.

Scene Eleven

MS. CHAN (*voice-over on the PA*)
The incident that took place in the cafeteria is being fully
investigated. Extra security guards will now work with Officer
Janice to monitor students in the hallways and cafeteria at all
times. Also: the junior volleyball team lost in the inner-city round
of sixteen, but put in a great effort, so congratulations. Go Trojans!

Scene Twelve

After school. Outside. BRIT is fired up. LILY is with her.

BRIT

Tenders tried to pin it on me. I said, "Since when do they own that table? What about our freedom?" After, I went to McDonald's with all of them. Me and Bennie and those two kids, the twins. You know, the ones with the moustaches? I was so pumped. It's normal for people to want to be with people who are the same as them. That's human nature. All the teachers and school BS always going "racism," "racism." That's because they're trying to take away our power. Why are all these people coming here?

LILY

It's because of, like, wars. They're trying to get a better life.

BRIT

Yeah, but we're not trying to get into their country. If there were, like, millions of us, moving into their schools, their neighbourhoods –

LILY

Millions?

BRIT

Just listen. If we were in their country, you think they'd be, like, "Hey, take all our stuff, do whatever you want"?

LILY

What about me? I'm not white.

BRIT

No, it's cool. I talked to Bennie. I told him, "She's adopted. Her mom and dad are Canadian." He said, "I get it." Okay? Bennie's really smart. Not, like, school smart, but actually smart. It's not about the colour of your skin. It's about, like, your way of life, and being with people who think like you.

LILY

Are you in love with him or something?

BRIT

No! That's not it at all.

LILY

What if I wasn't adopted? What if I had a Vietnamese family and we were immigrants? A lot of Vietnamese people were refugees, a long time ago. There was, like, this war, that we started against them. And then thousands of them had to escape on boats. Would Bennie say he gets it then? Would you even want to be my friend?

BRIT

Look, I didn't want to say anything, but the twins were talking. They heard Karim telling some of the Muzzies about this thing he's making, some kind of weapon.

LILY

No way, // Brit.

BRIT

It's what // they said.

LILY

That's crazy.

BRIT
You don't know him, Lil. You don't know any of them, what they're capable of. None of us do. Because they're different. It's not their fault, but they are. Besides, he's just a guy. There's tons of guys. Like the twins. They're cool.

LILY
They have moustaches.

BRIT
They're into *Star Wars*.

> *Beat.*

LILY
Brit, we need to talk –

BRIT
We are talking. And this is really important. We're best friends. Right?

> *Beat.*

LILY
Right.

BRIT
So trust me, okay? For real. Do you trust me?

LILY
... Yes.

BRIT
Good.

Beat.

LILY texts.

BRIT
Who are you texting?

LILY
Nobody.

BRIT
Oh, I forgot to tell you. Last night, when you bailed, my mom told me that she'd lost her job.

LILY
She did?

BRIT
Yeah, a while ago actually. I guess she was hiding it from me.

LILY
Brit.

BRIT
It's okay. It's fine. Going to need some money for rent. Maybe you could ask your parents. Don't say why, though. I don't want to get sent into care.

LILY
Yeah. Brit, of course.

Music.

Scene Thirteen

*The Hill, overlooking the school. **LILY** is waiting as **KARIM** arrives. At some point he puts down his backpack.*

LILY
I'm glad you texted me back.

KARIM
Yeah.

LILY
It took a while.

KARIM
I needed some space.

LILY
I'm so sorry, Karim. About the caf, all of it. It's so messed.

KARIM
Yeah.

LILY
I didn't know what to do. Brit's changed.

KARIM
Really?

Beat.

LILY

We were in grade eight when her dad left. It was partly good, because he was kind of sketchy. Not bad but he'd, like, disappear for weeks with no explanation. I was with her when she found out. In this park we always used to go to. He just showed up out of nowhere. She was so happy to see him, basically ran across the playground. But then I could see something was wrong. She went to hug him but he barely moved. After a couple of minutes, he walked away. She turned back at me and I could see the tears on her face. I waved. She just left. Didn't answer her phone for three days. She never saw him again.

KARIM

Yeah, well, my parents came here because they didn't want to die in a war.

Beat.

KARIM

That's not true. My parents came because they wanted good jobs, a house, more money. They wanted that stuff for me.

Beat.

KARIM

Last year, when that pile of refugee kids arrived at once, they put their lockers together, just down the hall from mine. A few times one of them tried talking to me in Arabic. I pretended I didn't understand what they were saying. I didn't want people to think I was one of them. Then one time I was in PE. Bennie was in the class, too. We were doing dodge ball. Half the class was playing and half of us were watching. This refugee kid – Tarek – kept getting hit. He didn't understand the rules. Bennie and a couple of guys who are good at it started pegging him with the ball on purpose, like, hard. Tarek got pissed and after a while he just lost it, started screaming at these guys in Arabic and whipping balls at them. But he's, like, super small and the guys just laughed, so the teacher sent him to the bench. He sat down right next to me. He looked at me. He was breathing hard and in Arabic he said, "You see what they were doing?" He was almost crying. I looked up and I made a choice. "Yeah, I did," I said. In Arabic. And I stuck out my hand and said, "I'm Karim." Tarek nodded and then we just sat there watching the game. That's when I realized. I don't care what other people think or say or post. I just don't.

LILY
I get it. I really do.

KARIM
I like you, Lily. I like you a lot. But I also know who I am.

BRIT arrives.

BRIT
What is this?

KARIM
(*to LILY*) And now it's time for you to decide who you want to be.

LILY
What's going on?

BRIT
I don't know. What's his name told the twins that I should come up and meet you here.

KARIM
So you'd see.

BRIT
See what?

KARIM
Lil, you have to step up. And be who you are. I'm tired of being the one who always has to stand up to hate. I can't do it for you.

LILY
I didn't ask you to do anything.

KARIM
I know. But I care about you. And you like me.

BRIT
No.

KARIM
Because you're *like* me.

BRIT
You think you're so fricking smart.

KARIM
(*to BRIT*) Shut up. (*to LILY*) You don't have to take her crap. She treats you like shit and you give her money. You actually pay her. Think about that, just for a second.

BRIT
What?!

LILY
Karim, what are you doing?

KARIM
She's a racist, Lily. You're too good for her. Stand up for yourself.

BRIT
That's it. This is done!

> *BRIT rushes KARIM. He takes his backpack and tries to run away. BRIT grabs the backpack to stop him from getting away. The bag opens, revealing some kind of plastic pipe and wiring. BRIT lets go of the bag.*

BRIT
What is that?

> *KARIM goes to shut the bag.*

KARIM
Nothing. Give it!

> *BRIT tries to get the bag.*

BRIT
(*to LILY*) In his bag. (*to KARIM*) Let me see.

KARIM
No!

LILY
Brit!

> *KARIM protects his backpack, pulling it away. BRIT tries harder.*

KARIM
It's nothing.

BRIT
There's wires! // It's a weapon! Jesus Christ!

KARIM

Don't touch me, it's my science.

BRIT

I told you. See, Lily, I'm not crazy.

KARIM

Don't be an idiot –

BRIT

They want to hurt us, people like him, they want to take away //
the things we love.

KARIM

I made it for you!

BRIT

Lily, let's go!

LILY looks at KARIM.

KARIM

Lily. Come with me.

LILY

No. Not right now. I can't.

KARIM runs out.

Scene Fourteen

LILY talks to the audience.

LILY

Brit was totally freaking out, but I didn't go with her. All I could think about was how Karim told her about the money, when I asked him not to. How he basically set me up, got her to come to the Hill without my consent. And then told me what I had to do.

But also how he's right. I do let Brit push me around. How in the caf, when they were yelling at each other and everybody was freaking, I just stood there, in-between. Like I'm a dumb magician's assistant, smiling like an idiot, while my body is sawed in two.

Then I got an email.

LILY gets an email. It is projected:

"Congratulations! We're very pleased to let you know that you are one of two winners to Comic Con's Teen Star Wars Fan Fiction Challenge! Get your best writing together – you're going to Comic Con California!!!"

Scene Fifteen

LILY talks to the audience.

LILY

It was third block. I had drama. We were working on lip-synchs.

The sound of a siren.

LILY

At first I didn't think anything of it. There's a fire station two blocks away, there's always sirens.

That's a lie. I knew exactly what it was. Then another, and another.

The sound of more sirens. Coming from every direction. Closer and closer.

PRINCIPAL TENDERS (*voice-over on the PA*)

Attention, all teachers. This is a lockdown. This is not a drill. Please stay calm and secure the doors to your classroom. The school is in lockdown.

LILY

Everybody went silent. A couple of kids started to cry. It felt like that thing that you always hear about. That you always wonder, what if it happens here?

PRINCIPAL TENDERS (*voice-over on the PA*)

Please stay calm. The police are on the way. The school is in lockdown.

LILY

Our teacher started singing this song, "Amazing Grace," and people started joining in. Everybody. Nerds, white kids, refugees, the Black kids, this kid Dan who says he's a communist. He was crying. A bunch of people were. Because singing the song together, not knowing what was going on, made everybody feel a little more safe.

We heard yelling. It was Karim. A crash against a door. An adult screaming, "Down on the ground! Down on the ground!"

And then Karim going, "I didn't do anything. I swear! Get your hands off of me! I didn't do anything!"

Brit reported it. She told the VP she thought she saw a weapon. He called the cops and by the time they got here everybody thought it was a bomb.

LILY reveals the object – a homemade lightsabre.

LILY

It was a present. Karim was making it for me. A lightsabre. To take to Comic Con in case I won.

Karim got expelled, at first. But then there was a big viral thing on social media, and even some newspaper articles. About how a Muslim kid got in trouble for making a lightsabre for this girl he'd liked for a long time. And how people were racist because they automatically assumed it must be a bomb. They even interviewed me. "How does it feel?" they asked. To know that your school got locked down and he got in so much trouble just because he did such a sweet thing for you?

Scene Sixteen

Downtown, outside a photo shoot. LILY is in full Rey outfit, with BRIT, who is dressed normally.

BRIT
They're, like, taking pictures of you or something?

LILY
I guess they want to, like, showcase me or something. For their Instagram or whatever.

BRIT
Cool.

LILY
Then they're taking me to the airport.

> *Beat.*

LILY
Your mom called my parents. Did she tell you?

> *BRIT shakes her head.*

LILY
She told them that she knows she needs help. That she wants them to help her get on different meds. That she knows it's been really hard on you.

BRIT
She has been acting kind of ... different.

LILY

My mom knows about this mental-health program. If your mom was in it, they'd pay your rent, and you wouldn't have to go into care.

BRIT nods.

LILY

It'd be something.

BRIT

I thought it was a weapon. I'm sorry, but I really did.

LILY

I know.

KARIM arrives.

LILY

Hey. Thank you for coming.

KARIM

You didn't say she'd be here.

LILY

I know but – I need to talk to both of you.

BRIT

How are you?

KARIM

Why do you care?

BRIT

I... I messed up, okay? I wasn't thinking. I'm sorry.

LILY pulls out something she's written and reads.

LILY
"The dreams came back. Every night. Rey saw herself standing over two corpses. Burned in half by her red lightsabre. She knew them. She knew she was dreaming, that there was still time. And a voice. Her own voice. 'Your destiny is your destiny, not anyone else's. You are here to understand who you are. Speak your truth. Say what you want. That is the only way to stop the pain.'"

I wrote that last night. I wrote it for both of you.

BRIT
It's good.

KARIM
It is.

LILY wields the lightsabre. It's awkward, nerdy.

BRIT
What is up?

KARIM
Yeah. This is weird.

LILY
I know. It is weird. Because I am weird. It's who I am. Because I'm in-between. Not one thing or the other, but in the middle. Which means I can see things, sometimes, that other people can't.

(*to KARIM*) Brit's my best friend. And you asked me to give that up. But I won't. I can't. No matter what she does. We've been through everything and I love her. But I never said that. I never told you, "I will care about her no matter what." So I'm telling you now. And just because she doesn't have money and fancy cars, it doesn't make her stupid.

KARIM
I never said she was stupid.

LILY
Yes, you did. But you're right about me. I haven't been honest about who I am. Not even to myself. (*to BRIT*) I'm not like you, Brit, in one big way. I'm not white. I don't know much about what that means yet, but I'm not. Karim didn't take me away from anyone. I like him. And the shit Bennie says? It's racist. Period. So, if he's who you want to be like, then ... I'll always care about you, Brit, but then I literally can't have you as my friend.

BRIT
I don't want to be like Bennie.

LILY
Good.

> *LILY does a move.*

KARIM
Dude.

BRIT
Seriously.

LILY
Shhh. I'm a nerd. That's never going to change.

> *LILY does another move.*

LILY
I want both of you in my life, and I want you both to want that, too. Like, to start over. Let the past go. Like Rey learns to in the story I wrote.

Beat.

LILY, BRIT, and KARIM look at each other. LILY drops the moves.

LILY
I know I can't make either of you want it. But it's what I want. What do you say?

KARIM and BRIT look at each other. BRIT shrugs.

BRIT
Okay.

KARIM
Maybe.

BRIT
I'm sorry.

KARIM
Yeah.

LILY
She's apologizing.

KARIM
I know. Okay. Got it.

Beat.

BRIT
Did you really get a scholarship to MIT?

KARIM
They promised me one when I graduate.

BRIT
I can't even imagine.

KARIM
I guess they saw all the stuff on social media and ... it is kind of weird.

BRIT
Yeah.

LILY
My bus. I gotta go.

BRIT
California.

KARIM
That's so sick.

LILY
I'll be back in five days.

KARIM
I hope you win.

BRIT
Me too.

LILY
Thanks. (*holding up the lightsabre*) Bringing this. For luck. Which is a little ironic, I guess, since it caused so much trouble.

Beat.

I'll text you when I'm back. Both of you.

BRIT
Okay.

KARIM
Yeah. Good luck.

LILY talks to the audience.

LILY
So that's it. What happened. The contest just finished. I didn't win. They said my writing showed promise, but some of it was a little clichéd. Whatever.

I did go swimming, at Venice Beach. That was cool. And I hooked up with this really hot California skater dude. I'm joking – I didn't! Heading home tomorrow. Don't know what's going to happen when I get back.

But, like I said, I wrote it all down. And I do want people to see it. Because it's how I figured out that the in-between is a real place. It's where I'm from. It could even be where we're all from, in some ways. And maybe it's not always such a bad place to be.

THE END

Acknowledgments

Thank you to the Banff Playwrights Lab, a project of the Banff Centre for Arts and Creativity and the Canada Council for the Arts, where I wrote an early draft, and also to Margo McLoughlin, Ted Little, and the Writer-in-Residence program at the McLoughlin Gardens in Courtenay, British Columbia. To the grade nine drama students at Westmount High School in Montréal for hanging out with me and talking to me about their school. I am also grateful to my friend David J. Smith for some key dramaturgical insights, and my agent Colin Rivers, who always makes invaluable contributions to my work. Finally, my thanks and love to my sons Zak and Oscar Youssef, who connected me to the real lives of teenagers, and my partner Amanda Fritzlan, whose work is all about young people, and is a constant source of inspiration, laughter, and surprise.

PHOTO: Kari Medig

MARCUS YOUSSEF is based on unceded Coast Salish Territory. His fifteen or so plays have been produced in multiple languages in scores of theatres in more than twenty countries across North America, Europe, and Asia, from Seattle to New York to Reykjavik, London, Venice, Hong Kong, Vienna, Athens, Frankfurt, and Berlin. Marcus is the recipient of Canada's most prestigious theatre award, the Siminovitch Prize for Theatre, for his body of work as a playwright, as well as Berlin, Germany's Ikarus Prize, the Vancouver Mayor's Arts Award, the Rio Tinto Alcan Performing Arts Award, the Chalmers Canadian Play Award, a Seattle Times Footlight award, the Vancouver Critics' Innovation award (three times), and the Canada Council Staunch-Lynton Award. Over the years he has also written for a half-dozen shows on CBC Radio and Television and a wide variety of Canadian print and web-based publications. Marcus co-founded the East Vancouver artist-run production studio Progress Lab 1422 and was the inaugural chair of the City of Vancouver's Arts and Culture Policy Council.

@marcusyoussef
mqlit.ca/category/marcus-youssef/

STUDY GUIDE

THE IN-BETWEEN

by Marcus Youssef

Study Guide created by Nitasha Rajoo

GRADE RECOMMENDATION

Grades nine and up

CONTENT ADVISORY

Explores mature themes
Contains moments of strong language
Deals with issues of oppression, including
racism and white supremacy

Production photos on pages 87 and 89 by Andrée Lanthier

ABOUT THE PLAY

Born in Vietnam, but adopted and raised by a white family in Canada, Lily has always felt "in-between." When conflict breaks out between Lily's working-class white best friend and privileged BIPOC boyfriend, she is forced to make big choices about who she is and whose side she's on. Like Youssef's international hit *Jabber*, seen by hundreds of thousands of young people across North America and Europe and winner of Berlin's Ikarus Prize, *The In-Between* brings humour, sensitivity, and a deft, authentic ear to the adult-sized conflicts young people must navigate as they enter their later teens.

CHARACTERS

- **Lily**: Vietnamese Canadian, adopted as a baby and raised by a white Canadian family
- **Brit**: white, lives with her low-income single mom
- **Karim**: Lebanese emigrant whose parents work in tech

All are fifteen- to sixteen-ish.

SETTINGS

- St. Mary's Secondary School, where an increasingly large group of Middle Eastern refugees has arrived over the last few years

- The Hill, a spot overlooking the school where kids hang out

- Brit's apartment

THEMES & MOTIFS

- Economic Inequality
- Social Justice
- Immigration
- Refugees
- Diversity and Assimilation

- Identity and Culture
- Power and Privilege
- Stereotypes and Perception

CHARACTER TRAITS

Brit: tough, funny, low income

Lily: nerd, cheerful, compassionate

Karim: smart, politically aware, financially privileged

DEFINITIONS

- **refugee**: a person seeking safety and shelter from danger to their personhood, as a result of war, persecution, economic insecurity, or other threats. Refugees are often forced to seek safety outside the countries they inhabit.
- **gaslighting**: a form of psychological manipulation intended to cause another person to doubt or question their own reality and even their sanity.
- **white supremacy**: the racist, unsubstantiated belief in the superiority of white people over people of other races. Also worth noting: race is an ideological construct, not a biological one.

- **nazi**: a member of the German National Socialist Party, which pursued a policy of extermination against those it deemed inferior based on a violent, antisemitic, racist, homophobic, and ableist fascist ideology.
- **terrorist**: a perpetrator of violence and intimidation upon a community, often for political purposes. This term has been disproportionately used to refer to people using the means available to them to resist state-sponsored terror.
- **immigration**: the process of moving permanently to one country from another.

INTERVIEW WITH THE PLAYWRIGHT MARCUS YOUSSEF

QUESTION: What motivated you to write this play?

ANSWER: As I write in my playwright's note to the play, I first began writing *The In-Between* in 2015 after becoming obsessed with the story of Ahmed Mohamed, a grade-nine student in Texas whose clock-making science project was mistaken for a bomb. A gawky fourteen-year-old science nerd inspires this reaction because of the associations the dominant culture makes based on the sound of his name, the colour of his skin, and his presumed religion. None of this is surprising, of course. But it is also flabbergasting. I then began to think about how different but equally ridiculous presumptions are projected onto low-income folks, based in this case on class. And then I hit on the central idea of the play itself, which really comes from a version of my own experience. It is the experience of a person who, for whatever reason, identifies with both sides of assumed binaries, and so feels like they don't know which side they're supposed to be on.

QUESTION: Which character do you identify with the most?

ANSWER: I identify with Lily, in that she sees herself as white but is not. This is an experience I grew up with as the mixed-race child of a white mom and an Egyptian dad who lived in mostly white areas. I identify with Karim, because he's a Middle Easterner who is very Canadian and also has parents who have well-paying professional jobs. My father was a banker and made a significant amount of money. I also identify with Karim's combined fear of and interest in the refugees in his school who have come from the Middle East. The character I identify least with is Brit. Her experience is the furthest from my own. What I do identify with is the way she has to take care of her mentally ill mother, something that is very hard and painful for a young person to do, especially one living in poverty. I also love that she's funny and smart.

QUESTION: Technology plays a significant role in the play. What role do you believe technology and social media play in the lives of young people?

ANSWER: That's a giant question. I believe technology and social media are integral to the lives of young people. They are their culture. If someone had asked me the same question about television when I was a teenager, I would have looked at them and wondered what was wrong with them. TV was just part of my life. It was where I got my information, where I went to relax, where I experienced stories that were a huge part of the life I shared with my friends (much less so with my parents). I try to write about social media in the lives of teenagers in that spirit – recognizing that it is part of the air they breathe and so a part of their culture. It is many things. It plays many roles. I have other questions about the systems of surveillance, predictive capitalism, and abuse that are social media's business model, but those are not central to this play.

QUESTION: Do you have a favourite moment in the play?

ANSWER: Oh, jeez. I like a lot of it – thankfully! Lily's story about seeing the magician saw his assistant in half. When I wrote that, I felt like I had articulated something I have felt for a long time in a way that is weird and funny and touching. I like it when Brit playfully makes fun of Lily's *Star Wars* writing, exposing its innocent sexuality. I like Karim's monologue about Tarek and the dodge-ball game Tarek got picked on in. There's something about dodge ball – it's so brutal, in a way. (I love dodge ball, for the record. And the only place I ever played it was in school.) I also like how Lily uses her *Star Wars* story to try to change the story of what happens in her real life. I think that's what I do for a living. (I could keep going ... sheesh ...)

QUESTION: What questions or reactions do you hope audiences leave with after watching the production?

ANSWER: I think the biggest things are:

1. The idea that our identities are not fixed – that we all experience being in-between things, whether that's race, or our friends, gender or class, or our parents. And the idea that being in-between might be a helpful way to imagine our relationship to the world and each other.

2. That conflict is complicated and that we all navigate conflict in ways that are imperfect, flawed, and defined by our own experience.

3. Finally, that all three characters have legitimate reasons for doing what they do, making the mistakes they make, and that they are all, in their own ways, trying to make things – their lives, their relationships – better. They don't always succeed, but they are legitimately trying. I think that is true for most human beings, most of the time.

PRE-SHOW QUESTIONS

1. What does *The In-Between* make you think of?
2. Do you have a friend who looks and believes differently from you? What impact does that have on you?
3. What kind of people go to Comic Con?
4. What is a refugee? What does a refugee look like? A white supremacist?
5. Have you sent an email or text in anger to a friend? How did you feel?
6. What does "privilege" mean?
7. Have you ever been described as something you are not? How does that affect your self-image? Identity? Worth?
8. Have you ever felt stuck in the middle? Can you describe how that feels?
9. Do you know where Afghanistan is? Syria? Lebanon? Could you find them on a map? Do you know what the current political climate is in these three countries? Use research methods to find what the sources of tension and conflict are.
10. As a student, what are your views on race relations in Canada? Do we have race issues? Expand on your view.

POST-SHOW QUESTIONS

1. What is the key message or take-away from the play?
2. What are five adjectives that you would use to describe Lily, Brit, and Karim?
3. What are the misconceptions we have about refugees?
4. What are the misconceptions we have about white supremacy?
5. What are your initial reactions about the play?
6. Do you feel a sense of belonging at school? Please describe.
7. What do "diversity," "equity," and "inclusion" mean to you?
8. What do we need to do to create a more welcoming environment for new students?
9. What can you do to be an anti-racist champion in your school?
10. Lily says she is "Canadian" – what does that mean to Lily? What does that mean to you?

ACTIVITY ONE

WHAT IS YOUR STORY?

After watching the show, put students into three groups. Give them one character each (Brit, Karim, or Lily) and get them to fill in the Role on the Wall figure (see appendix). They should come up with as many words as possible that link to the facts and ideas about the character. These can include things the students know about their character, such as their appearance, age, and gender, as well as speculations such as what the character might like or dislike, who their friends or enemies are, or their dreams, ambitions, or secrets.

As an extension: Outside the Role on the Wall figure, students could place ideas about how other people view the character.

> **Role on the Wall** is a drama technique that allows students to infer meaning about a character's relationship between characteristics (emotions) and actions (behaviours) onto a simple outline of a human figure. By inviting students to analyze context clues, the group collectively explores and constructs a more complex understanding of a character's motivations.

Prompt questions for **Role on the Wall** to dive deeper into characterization:

1. What events, people, or actions impact this character?
2. Does the character ever change?
3. Who in the play has an opinion about the character?
4. How does the character feel as a result of these opinions?
5. Who are people the character looks up to? Looks down on? Why?

ACTIVITY TWO

MONOLOGUE WRITING

1.
> **LILY**
> I'm Canadian.
>
> **LILY**
> My parents are both white. I was adopted.

2.
> **BRIT**
> You look like your ancestors. You shouldn't go to Comic Con as Rey. You should go as a Chinese rice farmer.
>
> **LILY**
> Vietnamese. Duh.

3.
> Definition of a monologue: a long speech given by a character in a play.

INSTRUCTIONS

Many times during the performance, Lily speaks directly to the audience in what is known as a direct-audience monologue. During the moments above, Lily is frustrated that her best friend Brit confuses her background, calling her Chinese when she is in fact Vietnamese, and that Karim makes false assumptions about her parents. Put yourself in Lily's shoes. How would she feel, what are her thoughts, what is the impact that Brit's and Karim's ignorance has on Lily's identity? What impact does it have on their friendship?

Continue Lily's train of thought as she directs her focus to the audience. After saying "Duh" and "I was adopted," what is she truly feeling? What does she want to say?

Write for ten minutes. Do not let your pen leave the page. Write fluidly. Do not worry about grammar, spelling, or phrasing. JUST WRITE. When you are done, read it back. What discoveries have you made about Lily? Be prepared to share back to the class.

ACTIVITY THREE

IMAGE CREATION

Still Image: A still image is a frozen picture which communicates meaning. It can provide insight into character relationships with a clear focus using space and positioning, levels, body language, and facial expression. Students are encouraged to exaggerate their body gestures and facial expressions. Remember, there is no talking in a still image! This drama activity takes active collaboration and team work. Students are encouraged to work with everyone in the class.

INSTRUCTIONS

Divide the class into three groups. They will use some of the ideas from activity one to complete this exercise. In your assigned group, you will create three still images that shows moment of the character's life. You are encouraged to dig deep and show moments that occur either before the play starts or scenes we do not see. Everyone in the group must be in each image.

For example:

Lily:
1. Being told she was adopted
2. Going to Comic Con for the first time
3. Asking her parents money for Brit's family

Want a challenge? Your group might think of a thought aloud that the character says in each image. Get into your still image first, allow the audience time to see the image, and then say your line out loud. Think about how you will say the line to get your message across.

A **thought-track** is when a character steps out of a scene to address the audience about how they are feeling. Sharing these thoughts provides a deeper insight into the character and this key moment.

ACTIVITY FOUR

This activity was excerpted from the study guide produced by Toni Lynn Hakem for the Geordie Theatre and is used with permission.

MEMES AND MEDIA LITERACY

Memes are prevalent in today's online society, but how do we know if they're real or fake?

Discuss media literacy with your students.

Once students have a more thorough understanding of media literacy, discuss memes with them. Some questions:
- What is a meme?
- What is the goal or objective of a meme?
- How can you tell if a meme is factual or not?
- What are characteristics of a meme?
- What are the consequences of fictional memes going viral?
- How can we counter the spread of fictional memes going viral?
- What types of experiences have you had with memes?
- Have you ever fallen for a fake meme? Do you remember what it was?
- If yes, what made it seem real to you?
- How did you find out it was fake?

When the discussion is complete, students can now create their own memes, but there's a catch!

Privately assign each student the task of creating a fake or real meme. For this activity to work, students must keep private what they have been assigned.

Students will then each create a meme based on *The In-Between* and one of its associated themes. If they were assigned "fake," they will make a fake meme, and inversely if they were assigned "real."

When they are done, each meme will be shown to the class, and students will have to determine if the meme is real or fake. The student who gets the most right wins!

EXTENSION ACTIVITY:
MY MEDIA CONSUMPTION

Now that students have a more thorough understanding of media literacy, will their media-consumption habits change? If so, how?

Ask each student to detail if and how their media consumption might change.

REFERENCES

White Privilege Conference Global – Toronto, "What Is White Privilege?," www.ryerson.ca/wpc-global/about/what-is-white-privilege/

Racial Equity Tools, "Racial Equity Tools Glossary," www.racialequitytools.org/glossary

APPENDIX

ROLE ON THE WALL FIGURE FOR ACTIVITY ONE

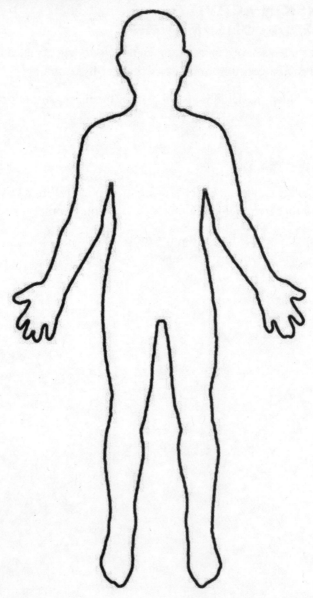